high-tech military weapons

MODERN BOMBS

Steve White

HIGH
interest
books

Children's Press®
A Division of Scholastic Inc.
New York / Toronto / London / Auckland / Sydney
Mexico City / New Delhi / Hong Kong
Danbury, Connecticut

Book Design: Erica Clendening
Contributing Editor: Geeta Sobha

Photo Credits: Cover by Mai/Mai/Time Life Pictures/Getty Images; p. 1 © Jayme Pastoriic/U.S. Navy/Getty Images; p. 3 courtesy of Lockheed Martin; p. 4 U.S. Air Force photo by Maj. David Kurle, 455 AEW/PA; pp. 6–7 U.S. Air Force courtesy photo; p. 8 © Hulton-Deutsch Collection/Corbis; p. 11 © Bettmann/Corbis; p. 12 © Corbis; p. 16 © 1999 Raytheon Company; p. 19 Mark Pahuta/U.S. Navy; p. 21 © Jason Frost/AP/Wide World Photos; p. 22 U.S. Air Force photo by Tech. Sgt. Michael Ammons; p. 23 U.S. Navy photo by Photographer's Mate Airman Jessica Davis; p. 26 © Felix Garza/U.S. Navy/Getty Images; p. 28 U.S. Air Force photo by Senior Airman Mike Meares; p. 30 © Scott Nelson/Getty Images; pp. 32–33 © Photo by U.S. Navy/Michael W. Pendergrass/Getty Images; p. 34 © photo by U.S. Navy/Getty Images; p. 36 © photo by USAF via Getty Images; p. 38 © David McNew/Getty Images

Library of Congress Cataloging-in-Publication Data

White, Steve, 1946-
Modern bombs / Steve White.
p. cm.
ISBN-10: 0-531-12093-7 (lib. bdg.)   0-531-18709-8 (pbk.)
ISBN-13: 978-0-531-12093-4 (lib. bdg.)   978-0-531-18709-8 (pbk.)
1. Guided bombs—Juvenile literature. I. Title. II. Series

UG1282.G8W47 2006
623.4'51-dc22
2006011897

1 2 3 4 5 6 7 8 9 10 R 11 10 09 08 07

CONTENTS

The Mark 82 bomb shown here is an ordinary bomb that can be fitted to a guided bomb unit. It weighs 500 pounds (227 kg).

Target confirmation, arm, and release consent!" You have just given the command to launch a bomb. You're in a control center on an airfield. It's early morning and you're sitting with a laptop computer on the table in front of you. The computer is showing a TV picture of a blue sea hundreds of miles away.

Another screen beside it shows the radar screen of an aircraft. On the radar, you watch a smaller airplane fly toward a town on the coast. These pictures are being beamed to you from hundreds of miles away as well. There's a beep. The bomb is 60 miles (97 kilometers) from the town. Among the quiet, sandy streets is a house in which some of the most dangerous terrorists in the world are sleeping. They are your targets. Still high out over the sea, the plane carrying the bomb opens its bomb bay. The plane is small, so is the weapon it is carrying.

The bomb falls away. It is on its back, but as it falls it rolls onto its front, and four wings

This photograph shows a laser-guided bomb (right) about to hit a barge.

pop out to form a diamond shape. These wings lift the bomb and allow it to glide to its target far away. High overhead, in space, a satellite guides the bomb toward the terrorists.

In this age of technology, bombs are being upgraded constantly. Bombers can do their jobs

from great distances, out of harm's way. How
do so-called smart bombs work? Read on to
find out how ordinary bombs got smart.

chapter 1

MAKING GRAVITY BOMBS SMART

The use of bombs goes back to the seventeenth and eighteenth centuries in Europe. Early explosive weapons were called grenades. They were small, round objects that were lit and thrown at enemies by special soldiers called grenadiers.

By the early twentieth century, bomb designs began to evolve and bombs got bigger. During World War I (1914–1918), bombs were thrown from airplanes onto enemy areas. They had shells that contained explosives and fins to keep them steady as they fell toward Earth.

This method of bombing was not very effective. Early aircraft had small engines, meaning they could only lift small bombs

Here, a German warplane drops an ordinary bomb. This bomb was too light to do any significant damage to the target.

that were not very powerful. In addition, many bombs often drifted off and missed their targets. As technology developed, improvements were made to bombs.

X MARKS THE SPOT

By the time World War II (1939–1945) erupted, airplanes were bigger and more powerful. Airplanes used for bombing were called bombers. The bombs, though, had hardly changed shape since they were first invented thirty years earlier—the bombs still looked like fat cigars with fins on the back to keep them steady as they dropped. Still, they were not steady enough. Winds could blow them off target, and flaws in their shape could cause them to drift off course as they fell. This was, of course, assuming they had been dropped correctly in the first place.

GRAVITY BOMBS

Most bombs were simply dropped on a target without any help or guidance. These are called gravity bombs because they depended on the force of gravity to pull them to their target. On approaching a target, the soldiers dropping the

This bomber called the B-17 Flying Fortress was used during World War II.

bombs had to figure out their distance from the ground and the target. They then had to drop the explosives within a specific time frame in order to hit the target. Hitting a target relied on the accuracy of calculations and many other elements.

Bombers usually flew hundreds, even thousands, of feet in the air, so seeing targets was often difficult. Targets could be hidden by

These bombs are being dropped from a B-29 bomber onto Kobe, Japan, in 1945.

smoke or clouds. Attacks carried out at night also presented visibility problems. Sometimes there were people on the ground shooting at the bombers. Even with better technology, hitting a target during World War II remained difficult. What was needed was a bomb that could hit a target accurately.

THE FIRST GLIDE BOMB

The first efforts to give a bomb a helping hand to find its target took place in World War II.

The Germans developed the first glide bomb, the Henschel Hs 293. The Hs 293 was basically a bomb with little wings like a plane that could be dropped 6 to 9 miles (10 to 14 km) away from its target and guided toward it by an operator on the bomber. Using a flare in the tail of the Henschel that showed its position, the operator guided it to the target by sending it radio signals to make course corrections.

The Hs 293 was used to destroy ships. On November 21, 1943, the Germans attacked a British convoy using the glide bombs for the first time. They successfully sank one ship and damaged another. Bombs had just gotten smarter, but there was still a long way to go.

ON POINT

After World War II, explosive weapons technology made great strides. Rocket science was used to create powered missiles. Bombs—explosives that are dropped over targets—were vastly improved as well.

By 1967, the U.S. Air Force (USAF) was using the Walleye glide bomb. This 1,000-pound (454 kilograms) weapon was guided to the target by a TV camera in its nose. The camera's picture was beamed back to a TV in the cockpit of the plane carrying the Walleye. The operator would center the target on a screen with crosshairs, "show" this point to the Walleye, then drop the bomb. The Walleye could be launched from 16 miles (26 km) away, keeping clear of antiaircraft guns and missiles. It would then glide down to the target.

BOMBS IN VIETNAM

During the Vietnam War (1954–1975), bridges were important targets. Two in particular came under attack many times: the Thanh Hoa and

MILITARY EXPLOSIVES

Missiles, like bombs, are explosive weapons used by the military. While bombs basically move with the help of gravity, missiles are carried by rockets or jet engines swiftly and directly to targets.

Missiles, like smart bombs, have fins to keep steady. In a missile, explosives are contained in a special section called a warhead. The warhead is released when the missile reaches the target.

the Paul Doumer bridges. These were huge steel structures that carried traffic and railway lines across rivers.

In April 1965, USAF bombers attacked the Thanh Hoa, called the "Dragon's Jaw" by the Vietnamese. Three hundred and twenty bombs and thirty-two missiles were launched at the bridge, but the Dragon's Jaw remained standing. The Paul Doumer Bridge was first attacked on August 11, 1967. A 3,000-pound (1,361 kg) bomb hit the bridge, destroying part of it. It was unusable for seven weeks.

Between 1965 and 1967, bombers from the USAF and U.S. Navy continued to attack the two bridges. They dropped hundreds of gravity bombs, fired dozens of missiles, and lost aircraft and aircrew in the process. Though both bridges were damaged, they were not destroyed.

The Paveway (bottom) proved to be a major advancement in bomb building.

chapter 2

BOMB KITS

Work on a more effective bomb continued. Between 1964 and 1965, a guidance kit that could be attached to a normal gravity bomb was developed. Thus, the first smart bomb was born. This first guidance kit contained a special seeker head that was attached to the nose of a 2,000- to 3,000-pound (907 to 1,361 kg) bomb. The kit also included fins to be fitted to the front and back of the bomb. The bigger fins at the back allowed the bomb to glide to its target. Those at the front were moveable and helped steer the bomb on the correct course. These laser-guided bombs (LGBs) were called Paveway (Pave stands for Precision Avionics Vectoring Equipment).

A laser beam was projected at a target from a pod attached to the plane carrying the bomb. Within the pod was a TV camera through which an operator on the plane could aim the laser at an exact spot on the target.

The bomb then used its seeker head to follow the reflection of the light to the target.

The LGB could be dropped from as far away as 8 miles (13 km)—much farther than any gravity bomb. The problem for the LGB was that the target had to be clearly visible. Clouds or smoke could scatter the laser's light. When this happened, the bomb's seeker head would not have enough light to follow.

LGBS AT WORK

Bombers carrying out LGB attacks had to operate in pairs. One carried the laser designator in a pod called Pave Knife. The second aircraft carried the bombs themselves, usually two of them. Today's aircraft can carry both the designator pod and the bombs. Testing on early versions of LGBs began in 1968 during the Vietnam War. Five were dropped in May, and they worked.

On May 10, 1972, eighteen bombers—including fourteen carrying LGBs and four carrying glide bombs—attacked the Paul Doumer Bridge. Twenty-two LGBs and seven glide bombs struck the bridge, leaving it badly

This Pave Knife designator pod (right) was used during the Vietnam War to deliver laser-guided bombs.

damaged. None of the aircraft were hit by the Vietnamese forces. The following day, eight 2,000- and 3,000-pound (907 and 1361 kg) LGBs were dropped, damaging the bridge beyond repair.

BREAKING THE DRAGON'S JAW

The Dragon's Jaw was attacked on April 27, 1972. However, LGBs could not be used due to cloudy weather. Instead Walleye glide bombs were dropped. These caused severe damage but did not destroy the bridge. The next crack at the Dragon's Jaw came on May 13. Fourteen

USAF bombers attacked in clearer weather. Twenty-four LGBs were dropped, along with glide bombs and gravity bombs. Enemy fire was heavy, but the bombers dropped their LGBs from a safe distance. The Dragon's Jaw was soon swallowed up by the smoke and fire of explosions. When the smoke cleared, the bridge had been destroyed.

PRECISION-GUIDED MUNITIONS

The attacks on the Thanh Hoa and Paul Doumer bridges proved that smart bombs were able to hit important targets accurately. Many air forces began using them. Smart bombs were to prove themselves again during the 1991 Gulf War. LGBs, which are also called precision-guided munitions (PGMs), were used to destroy important targets such as bridges and command centers. PGMs include all types of weapons that use guidance systems.

Even so, only 7 percent of the smart bombs dropped in the Gulf War (1990–1991) were PGMs. By the start of the Iraq War in 2003, that number has risen to 65 percent! PGMs allow the soldiers using them to hit targets from a safe distance.

These are 2,000-pound (907 kg) precision-guided bombs that were used in the Iraq War in 2003.

The first Paveway led to the development of the technology for these PGMs. The modern USAF now has many types of PGMs in use, showing how far the technology has come since the first LGBs were dropped in Vietnam.

chapter 3

BUILD A BETTER BOMB

ollowing the success of Paveway LGBs in Vietnam, efforts quickly got underway to advance bomb technology. The Paveway II and Paveway III were bomb kits that had better seeker heads with wider viewing areas. They are called guided bomb units (GBUs). The Paveway II was developed in the 1970s, followed by Paveway III in the 1980s. The Paveway III kit could be used to upgrade ordinary bombs and penetrator bombs. Penetrator bombs are smart bombs that can find their way into hard-to-reach areas.

There are several types of Paveway II:

- **GBU-10**: This version uses a 2,000-pound (907 kg) bomb. There are two types–the ordinary GBU-10 and the GBU-10I, which fits an LGB kit to a BLU-109B

This GBU-12 is lighter than the GBU-10. This makes it easier for planes to carry. These bombs were used to destroy tanks during the Gulf War in 1991.

A member of the USAF inspects a GBU-16 Paveway I smart bomb

bomb designed to blast targets hidden underground or protected by concrete.

- **GBU-12**: This is a 500-pound (227 kg) bomb fitted with an LGB kit. This version uses a plastic seeker head instead of metal to make it lighter and folding fins that make it easier for a plane to carry them. GBU-12s were dropped in the Gulf War, where they were used to destroy tanks, hitting 88 percent of their targets.
- **GBU-16**: This is an LGB kit fitted to a 1,000-pound (454 kg) bomb.

As enemies' defense capabilities improved, bomb technology had to be developed to overcome these defenses. In 1986, the Paveway III–the GBU-24 Low-Level Laser Guided Bomb (LLLGB)–was introduced. It can be dropped from very low altitudes and from farther away than other LGBs. Pilots use a loft attack to do this. In a loft attack, the aircraft pulls quickly upward at a certain point and releases the bomb. The bomb then glides to the target.

The GBU-24B/B is a penetration Paveway III that is made with a thick casing around the bomb to punch through 4 to 6 feet (1 to 2 meters) of concrete. A major improvement in Paveway III bombs is their ability to make adjustments on their own to reach a target.

GUIDED BOMB UNIT-15

The GBU-15 is a kit like that of an LGB that can be fitted to general purpose or penetrator bombs. The difference is that the GBU-15 uses TV guidance instead of a laser. It is guided to the target by an electronic signal called a data link. It can reach 5 or more miles (8 km) farther than a laser-guided bomb.

The F-14D Tomcat fighter jet is equipped with a 500-pound (227 kg) laser-guided bomb.

The GBU-15 does not need to see its target before being dropped. The operator can point it in the general direction of the target and then use the TV camera in its nose to find it. The bomb can then be steered using the data link to the aim point. The GBU-15 also has a heat-detecting infrared TV camera, which means it can find targets at night or in bad weather.

The GBU-15 kit has five parts, including the guidance section fitted with the TV cameras that are fixed to the nose and the data link that is fitted on the bomb's tail. There are also four wings to help guide the bomb.

This GBU has two methods of attack: direct and indirect. With the direct method, the operator chooses the target for the bomb before it is dropped. The guidance system locks onto the target and then the weapon is launched. The bomb guides itself to the target without any help. In an indirect attack, the bomb is dropped and then guided by the operator to the target, using the data link. In the Gulf War, seventy-one GBU-15s were dropped.

A new version, the EGBU-15 (the E stands for enhanced), came into use in 1999. It uses the same TV guidance as satellites in space to help it find a target–this is called the Global Positioning System (GPS). With GPS, the EGBU-15 can find a target completely hidden in clouds or fog and make a hit. The EGBU-15 also has a range of 15 miles (24 km).

HIDDEN TARGETS

Many important targets are buried underground, making them hard to destroy. Penetrator bombs that can reach these hidden targets are important in today's warfare. They can destroy enemies without risking the lives of soldiers.

An air force sergeant uses a special piece of equipment to move the 5,000-pound (2,268 kg) GBU-28.

GBU-28 BLU-113 PENETRATOR

The GBU-28 was designed to punch through 100 feet (30 m) of earth or 20 feet (6 m) of concrete. Work began on this bomb in 1990 when Iraq invaded Kuwait, sparking the Gulf War. Iraq hid many important weapons and soldiers underground. The USAF needed a new weapon that could get by the Iraq defenses.

The tube of an army cannon was used for the body. It was then fitted with an LGB kit. Its 19-foot-long (6 m) body was partly buried in the ground. Specially trained workers packed explosives into the bomb outside a laboratory in New York. The first two bombs weighed 4,700 pounds (2,132 kg) each. They were sent to the USAF for testing. On February 27, 1991, the bombs were rushed to the Persian Gulf, where the war had already begun. Both were dropped, destroying their targets.

BOMB FACTS

The North Atlantic Treaty Organization (NATO) used GBU-28 penetrator bombs in 1999 during the conflict in Kosovo. This province of Serbia had been struggling for independence from the ruling government.

A 2,000-pound (907 kg) JDAM bomb strikes its target in Fallujah, Iraq, causing much destruction.

chapter 4

THE FUTURE: SMART TO BRILLIANT

Being able to reach a target from the farthest point, both on the ground and in the air, is one of the most important features of smart bombs. The newest smart bombs employ the latest technology to hit targets accurately. The following shows just how some of these bombs work.

JDAM (JOINT DIRECT ATTACK MUNITION)

This is a tail kit that can be fitted to most general purpose and penetration bombs used by the USAF and U.S. Navy. The JDAM can be dropped from a wide range of altitudes and can reach targets 15 miles (24 km) away. The tail unit includes a GPS and an Inertial Navigation System (INS). Bombs using it can be guided to their targets by the INS, which is a computer system that marks places using two

sets of numbers called coordinates. A JDAM can be dropped at night or in bad weather and still hit a target by following these numbers.

The details of a JDAM mission, such as when it will be dropped or where the target is,

Aboard the USS *Harry Truman*, GBU-31 JDAMs are ready to be fitted onto fighter jets.

are entered into the bomber's computer. On the way to the target, the plane's computer uploads this information onto the bombs. Even if many JDAMs are dropped from the same aircraft in one attack, each JDAM can hit a

The crew of the USS *Carl Vinson* load a JSOW on an F/A-18 Hornet in preparation for a mission.

different target.

There are several versions of JDAM, all with the same tail kit and small fins that improve the bomb's agility. Many have been dropped during the Afghan and Iraq campaigns.

AGM-154 JSOW (JOINT STAND-OFF WEAPON)

The JSOW is a new glide bomb that can be launched 40 miles (64 km) from its target at high altitudes, 15 miles (24 km) at low altitudes. This bomb was developed in the late 1990s. It uses GPS-aided INS like the JDAM. The JSOW is 13 feet (4 m) long and weighs between 1,000 and 1,500 pounds (454 and 680 kg), depending on its load. It was first used in battle in 1998 in attacks on Iraq. During the Kosovo conflict in 1999, JSOWs scored 100 percent accuracy against targets. There are three versions of JSOW.

- **AGM-154A**: This is a general purpose JSOW. It carries 145 BLU-97/B small bombs that have different types of explosives to attack different kinds of targets.
- **AGM-154B**: This version uses six BLU-108/B small bombs to attack tanks and

A Boeing small diameter bomb has been mounted on the wing of a USAF F-15E Strike Eagle.

other armored vehicles. Each one carries four smaller bombs, which can detect a target vehicle's heat. When the target is detected, the bomb explodes, shooting a slug of armor-defeating explosives into the target.

- **AGM-154C**: This version has a heat-seeking TV and a data link for an operator to guide to the target. It also uses a BROACH (bomb royal ordnance augmented charge) warhead that has two separate explosives that can either blow up together or one after another. The first punches a hole in the target. The second one enters the target then explodes inside it.

SMALL DIAMETER BOMB (SDB)

The size of small diameter bombs (SDBs) allows one aircraft to carry many of them. The size also enables bombers to use it against targets surrounded by civilians. For example, SDBs can be used on a terrorist hideout on a busy street. The target would be destroyed without hurting civilians in the area around it.

There are two types of SDBs. The first version uses GPS-aided INS to find stationary targets, such as buildings, fuel tanks, and command centers. The second type of SDB uses a heat-detecting seeker head that has a computer that can recognize different types of vehicles.

The SDB weighs only 250 pounds (113 kg), but its 50-pound (23 kg) warhead is able to punch through 6 feet (2 m) of concrete. To increase the bomb's range, the SDB uses a Diamond Back Precision-Attack Gliding Kit. When the bomb is dropped, it rolls onto its front. The wings stored in its back pop open to form a diamond shape. The Diamond Back increases the range of the SDB to 60 miles (97 km). The wings can even drop off during the glide so the bomb can pick up speed before hitting its target.

At Edwards Air Force Base, the USAF unveils two X-45A UCAVs to the news media.

SMART TO BRILLIANT

As technology improves, weapons will continue to get smarter. Eventually they will be so smart that the human element can be completely removed from the picture. Electronic warfare has become more important than tanks, planes, or ships. As computers become increasingly smaller and more powerful, so will weapons. The power of electronics and computers has sped up warfare. Computers fight far faster than people do.

Bombs such as SDBs are just the beginning of a new range of weapons. The smaller bombs of tomorrow will have all the explosive power of today's larger weapons. They will not even need lasers or TV cameras to guide them. Their computer brains will do all the thinking. The computer will find the target and work out the best to way to reach and destroy it.

Aircraft will become bomb trucks, which will just be a way of getting the bombs into a target area. Many of these aircraft will soon be without humans inside them. Unmanned aerial vehicles (UAVs) and unmanned combat aerial vehicles (UCAVs) will replace warplanes flown by pilots. Soon a bombing mission will involve a robot plane flying itself on a mission to drop a bomb that will find its own way to its target–all without any help from a human.

GBU-32 JDAM
Joint Direct Attack Munition

At a Glance

Strakes

MK83 warhead

Fin

AFT GPS antenna

Tail assembly

GPS / INS guidance kit

GENERAL CHARACTERISTICS

PRIMARY FUNCTION: CLOSE AIR SUPPORT, NAVAL ANTI-SURFACE WARFARE, AMPHIBIOUS STRIKE, SUPPRESSION OF ENEMY AIR DEFENSE	RANGE: UP TO 15 MILES (24 KM)
GUIDANCE: GLOBAL POSITIONING SYSTEM / INERTIAL NAVIGATION SYSTEM	CONTRACTOR: BOEING (MCDONNELL DOUGLAS AEROSPACE)
LENGTH: 120 INCHES (304 CM)	WEIGHT: 1,015 POUNDS (460 KG)
WEAPONS: MK83 WARHEAD	COST: $18,000

NEW WORDS

bomber (**bom**-ur) a military aircraft designed to drop bombs

civilian (si-**vil**-yuhn) someone who is not a member of the armed forces

crosshairs (**krawss**-hairz) *x* or + shape on a bombsight used to aim at a target

data link (**day**-tuh **lingk**) electronic signal between two places, such as a plane and a guided bomb ·

gravity bomb (**grav**-uh-tee **bom**) a bomb that relies on gravity to hit a target

infrared (**in**-fruh-red) relating to the invisible part of electromagnetic spectrum

laser (**lay**-zur) a device that makes a narrow, powerful beam of light

operator (**op**-uh-ray-tur) a person who uses and controls mechanical instruments

NEW WORDS

pod (**pod**) long narrow case used by aircraft to carry things in

radar (**ray**-dar) from radio detecting and ranging; a device that sends out radio waves that reflect off objects back to the sender and onto a display screen

seeker head (**seek**-ur **hed**) part of a smart bomb, usually on the nose, that finds the signal to guide it to the target

smart bombs (**smart bomz**) bombs that can guide themselves to a target by following signals from a laser, satellite, or TV camera

technology (tek-**nol**-uh-**jee**) use of science and engineering to do practical things

unmanned aerial vehicle (un-**mand air**-ee-uhl **vee**-uh-kul) an airplane or helicopter that has no pilot and is controlled from the ground

FOR FURTHER READING

Evans, Anthony A. *Modern Attack Planes: Aircraft, Weapons and Their Battlefield Might.* London: Greenhill Books, 2004.

Miller, David, ed. *The Illustrated Directory of Modern American Weapons.* Osceola, WI: Motorbooks International, 2002.

Pustam, Anil R. *Modern Bombers: Aircraft, Weapons and Their Battlefield Might.* London: Greenhill Books, 2004.

RESOURCES

ORGANIZATIONS

Smithsonian National Air and Space Museum
Independence Avenue at 4th Street, SW
Washington, DC 20560
www.nasm.si.edu

U.S. Air Force
1500 Army Pentagon
Washington, DC 20310-1500
www.airforce.com

RESOURCES

WEB SITES

BBC NEWS SMART BOMBS

*http://news.bbc.co.uk/1/hi/world/americas/
2805577.stm*
This site provides graphics showing how smart bombs work.

HOW SMART BOMBS WORK

http://science.howstuffworks.com/smart-bomb.htm
This site has photographs and interesting facts about smart bombs.

SMART WEAPONS

*www.globalsecurity.org/military/systems/
munitions/smart.htm*
For older readers, this site has a lot of technical information and many photos.

INDEX

INDEX

ABOUT THE AUTHOR
Steve White currently edits *Wallace & Gromit*
and *Best of The Simpsons* for Titan Comics. In his
spare time, he continues to develop his obsession
with sharks, dinosaurs, and *The Simpsons*.